101 Things to do Naked!
A Guide to 'Dress-Free' Living

By Catherine Roberts

Illustrations by Mike Dominic

Table of Contents

Not all the Greek runners in the original Olympics were totally naked.
Some wore shoes. ~ Mark Twain

Introduction

Back in the day (not ours, the first Olympians), Thucydides argued that nudism elevated the Greeks above the fur-clad barbarians. Not something I always agreed with. Over time and circumstance however, my musings on the subject created a significant shift in attitude. I went from modern-day me, assuming the daily ritual of dressing was a civilized occurrence, to not giving a fig about being naked.

Eventually, I discovered that I was a born naturist. Turns out we all are. Seems I've always enjoyed moments of solitude, where I could indulge in any given task, without the encumbrance of clothing. Apparently, I'm not alone. Throughout humankind's descent into modern times, countless persons of note, as well as mere mortals, have defied the status quo and stood their ground – naked!

How is this so? Well, as I'm going to demonstrate, nudity can be enjoyed in a multitude of ways. In fact, its only limitations should be dictated by maturity, common sense, and self-preservation. For example, cooking, a most enjoyable activity most of the time, can be done in the nude. But, frying bacon naked really should be avoided. Hot flying fat hurts . . . trust me. And finally, nudity changes the way you look at things and yourself. You lighten up. Living naked makes you feel a little bolder, a little freer, a lot more aware . . . and hopefully, a lot less like a fur-clad barbarian.

So sling a towel under your bare bottom (if you're sitting on the 'good' furniture), set your feet up on the coffee table and settle in. We've barely begun . . .

Preface

Rediscovering the joy of being naked

Remember 8-millimeter film? I'm the star attraction in one of our family's earliest home movies. Unbeknownst to me, it portrays yours truly running around an airport tourist attraction – a post-war monument – a B52 Bomber, in fact – running shamelessly around . . . naked! Aunt Dot leaked this lovely tidbit of information at a family reunion during a deluge of nostalgic tale telling. Ok, I admit that at two years of age there must have been countless times that I shimmied out of my skivvies and ran around with wild abandon. It probably happened as habitually and as naturally as a gecko shedding its skin.

No doubt as well, we all have stories of appropriate (and sometimes not so appropriate) nudism that sort of lumps us all together and distinguishes us as mortal beings. After all, don't we all come into this world the same way each and every time? To my knowledge, nary a soul has been born pre-clad in a terrycloth sleeper – pink or blue!

Pop-psychology tells us that the toddler era ends around the time that we become embarrassed about being seen in our bare asses. So in the process of growing up, we learn to shroud ourselves in leather, furs and textiles synthesized from all sources known to man – natural and otherwise.

Today, I'm absolutely charmed knowing that in our family movies there are none with me wearing clothing . . . ever! Interestingly, by the time I scooted into my threes, the novelty of 8-millimeter film had worn off. Still-pictures became the norm, and to satisfy the status quo, all depict me in dresses, jumpers, jeans and other stitched up items you might find in a gal's dresser drawers and her 'never-enough' closet space.

Now, what amazes me about the home movies is not so much that I was being filmed naked as a toddler. It's that the joy I once found in being nude has found its way into my life once more, at an age when most people find themselves renovating, or building dream homes to include walk-in closets that will hold an exorbitant amount of leather, furs and textiles synthesized from all sources known to man – natural and otherwise.

The change occurred with my introduction to cottage life . . . on a warm spring morning. I woke to the sound of a cold steel wedge striking a cylindrical piece of birch. Thunk! Further investigation revealed my husband, Jay – ax in hand – methodically chopping wood. He wore sage green rubber boots . . . nothing more. I was, simply put, in awe! Sweat poured down his back, attesting to the arduousness of the chore. Clothing would have been a hindrance. It was then that it occurred to me. There must be a hundred more things you can do naked!

The seed was planted. Over the next four seasons it grew and blossomed. Today, in a world of 'how-to' handbooks, this is the one that teaches you what you already knew as a child – that almost everything you do is better with no clothes on. I say almost everything, as there are occasions when an activity done in the nude is detrimental to one's health – and we discourage that.

Basically my wife was immature. I'd be in my bath and she'd come in and sink my boats. ~ Woody Allen

March

Chapter One

Early spring, just before black fly season – the most dreadful time of year for die-hard cottagers and naked people everywhere. Especially in Nova Scotia. Being a human smorgasbord to those bloodthirsty pests is no picnic. In cottage country there simply is no greater irritation. Unless you count the calendar-challenged June bugs that appear in May, the mosquitoes that follow and, as well, the horse, deer and moose flies, which rear their progressively larger heads into the latter part of summer.

Never mind. By September nothing will be left of all those carnivorous beasts save a layer of scar tissue laid thick from incessant scratching. Come March, come early spring, come longer days and shorter nights, before those dreadful black flies appear, we shed our clothes to expose a fresh layer of epidermis, of our most expansive organ, of newly grown skin.

This is our time to shine . . . or, in this case, to start spring cleaning. Getting all the dirty deeds done now frees up time to do things we really enjoy during the longer, lazy, hazy days of summer.

Number one then on the list is *cleaning* (1). As long as it has to do with a cloth, some rags, a sponge or scrub brush and a polishing or cleansing agent, the terminology is a moot point. Just get it done. Scour those kitchen appliances, polish that silverware, clean out the china cabinet, the basement, the attic, and yes, the garage. Hose down the car, the siding on your house, the driveway, your long-ears-dragging-in-the-muddy-snow-all-winter-long hound dog. Squeegee your windows.

Just remember that all that dirt and grime has to go somewhere and, wearing clothes, chances are that ninety eight per cent of it will land on you. So, unless you want to spend the rest of the season doing laundry, do your spring cleaning in the nude.

Next is something that simply allows us to enjoy doing number one all the more – *singing* (2). Whenever I clean, the chore is infinitely more tolerable when I'm listening to music and singing my heart out. Pay no attention to that wretched howling going on in the background. It's just Blue, our Beagle, joining in the chorus.

March is also a fantastic time for *chopping wood* (3) – not too hot and, most importantly, no flies.

While my husband Jay swings his ax, I take the opportunity to stake out a plot for our cottage garden and take to *tilling* (4). Tinkering in the garden plot, I'm happy to see that the compost has successfully morphed into a rich, nutrient-dense soil. There're even worms! I'll put them in beds and have all my rows seed-ready for after the last frost warning. Pre-June would be nice.

In the meantime, Mr. Take-care-of-your-tools-and-your-toys-or-you-won't-have-any, is doing a *tune up* (5) on the four-wheeler, topping up battery fluid and checking the tire pressure. Tuning up leads to fun on the all-terrain vehicle and *four wheeling* (6) is one of our favorite things to do in the nude on our private trails in the forest.

If you lack private trails, take heart. Crown land will do just fine. Mid-week, a naked person on an ATV barreling down a trail that runs adjacent to the highway would raise barely an eyebrow in these parts.

Come the weekend, cottage country fills up, and you may attract more of an audience. Just wave and smile. Most folks will do the same. That's human nature. Of course, if you attract the attention of law enforcement, you may want to get your ass and your four-wheeler out of sight and parked on a private lot. At this point, if they still want to talk to you, try number seven on the list and *run* (7).

Running naked isn't something that we do a lot of. We do run recreationally and have managed a few half-marathons for charity, but the running we do in cottage country consists mostly of chasing each other around with bug zappers and fish heads – mostly childish antics that do not require us to be clad in sports bras and spandex pants.

A word or two on streaking and flashing: *Streaking became fashionable in the 70's primarily on university campuses and at major sporting events. Flashing is an act of perversion.*

We end March with a prayer that the coming months will bring fair weather. Nothing puts a damper on being naked like an overabundance of rain. Yes, we need some for the garden and to keep the water level up in the lake for recreational activities, but too much can be downright depressing. Makes me want to wrap myself in rubber. So we *pray* (8) . . . for just enough rain and plenty of sun.

*Being naked approaches being revolutionary; going barefoot
is mere populism. ~ John Updike*

April

Chapter Two

Shaded crevices house the last remnants of snow come April. The rivers run high, the kayaks beckon . . . the air is warm, the water chilly. We take advantage of the spring swell, as it doesn't last. The mighty Musquodoboit (pronounced musk-a-dah-butt) will retreat to a trickle and the swift Stewiacke River will slowly succumb to the relentless sun to reveal its ruddy-red underbelly.

Kayaking (9) naked is easier said than done when you delve into public waters. For the most part, launching areas are dangerously open to anyone who cares to look. Once we're underway though and out of view, we can doff our duds. This can be tricky business on a fast flowing river. Like walking across a trampoline with your eyes closed, one wrong wobble and whoops . . . down you go!

The thing about paddling down a river naked is that at some point you have to find your way back. Again, the trick is to get dressed without tipping yourself over. You want to be in the public eye now as you're 15 miles or so from your launch site. The only thing you want to have protruding and naked in this case is your thumb . . . pointed in the direction where you left your mode of transport. Until that time, however, there is nothing as tranquil as guiding your kayak downriver on a sunny spring day, nudged along by a gentle wind, clad only in the skimpiest of life jackets.

At the cottage, the very next morning, I wake to the aroma and sizzle of bacon frying. Yes, it is on my list of things to 'not' do naked, but tell that to my frying-in-the-face-of-danger husband. Jay scoffs at peril, disses aprons, and actually looks kind of cute dodging hot pork fat spitting out from a cast iron frying pan. Suffice it to say that *cooking* (10) is a major activity that one may engage in with no clothes on . . . at home or at the cottage.

'I'll butter the toast.'

With breakfast out of the way, my partner sets to *fixing stuff* (11). The chainsaw blade needs sharpening, a burner on the barbeque is clogged and the oarlock on the rowboat needs to be replaced. All will be taken care of with nary more on than a look of astute concentration. Seems to be the perfect time for me to do a little warm-up *yoga* (12) on my lotus mat.

Downward dogs aside, stretching in the nude and contorting the body into a myriad of unnatural shapes can be a lot of fun. Especially if done with a friend.

'Okay, move over mutt, the mat is mine!'

Now, as I'm quite the multi-tasker, I perform my Sun Salutations whilst *meditating* (13). This way, the other two activities I've committed to, but can't fathom why I did, become a little less daunting. Well okay, I admit, *painting* (14) the woodshed and *staining* (15) the deck are jobs I take on earnestly as I like the esthetic effect. And, as it's a week day with no curious neighbors around, I can leave my work duds hung inside the cottage. Coveralls are for sissies I've learned to say.

With all the kayaking, fixing, painting and staining done, someone is longing for attention. We can justify *taking the hound for a walk* (16), sans clothing, and switch up the rubber boots to dirt-road friendly flip flops.

'Ears up . . . good boy!'

"We was always naked, day and night, whenever the mosquitoes would let us." ~ Huck Finn
- Mark Twain's river hero

May

Chapter Three

April showers bring May flowers, Mother's Day, and grass . . . lots and lots of grass! By mid-May, Jay has cut the lawn and the camp grass more than a couple of times. He now has a good start on an all over bronzing with nary a tan line in sight. While hubby *mows* (17) and *rakes* (18), I get down and dirty in the garden. Planting a garden in the nude is for me the next best thing to meditation for rejuvenating the mind. It's also a great activity for achieving an even, line-free tan. Granted, it is less stressful to do at the cottage.

Gardening (19) naked in an urban area has its challenges . . . but, don't despair. I have found that a large brimmed straw hat and a few strategically held hand tools allow just the shred of decency you need to be outside planting a garden within the city limits. And, if that solution doesn't work for you, a privacy fence in the back yard does the job perfectly well.

Apartment dwellers who have outside patios needn't bother to cover any body parts unless they're on the first few floors facing a parking lot. Who would notice anything amiss 20 stories high while the world below speeds by? No one. Just fill a bunch of pots and planters with good quality garden soil and plant your little heart out. In a couple of weeks even the ground floor dwellers will be able to toss the tools and sun bonnets, as they'll be strategically covered by a plethora of sweet pea vines, gay gladiolas and comely cosmos.

When my husband and I finish yard work in the country, we reward ourselves with an outing to Sand Lake. Here we do a little trout *fishing* (20) and a little *bird watching* (21). More explicitly, the man does the fishing and the woman watches the birds. Even more explicitly, I have a hard and fast rule that states, 'you killed it – you clean it.' Hence, I do not fish. If this admission gives the impression that when it comes to bloody guts I'm a gigantic sissy, then so be it. Guilty as charged.

Now, while big boy slices those long, shiny bodies back at the cottage, I take my mind off the carnage by taking a cool outdoor *shower* (22). The air is balmy for May and in answer to our prayers, we've had moderately wet weather, which has the garden swelling with pride, shoots and some leafy stuff I don't quite recognize . . . hmmm.

No matter. We have a couple of hours to kill before the sun goes down. We'll *pedal* (23) down a trail on our mountain bikes, keeping just ahead of the flying vampires. Yes, the black flies and mosquitoes have found us to be delightfully tender. Drat, scratch . . . fever!

Fashion is a form of ugliness so intolerable that we have to alter it every six months. ~ Oscar Wilde

June

Chapter Four

Summer . . . glorious summer has arrived. This is our favorite time of year. Our tans are now becoming deep and, not surprisingly, even. It's when we take every opportunity to wear little more than smiles and *bask* (24) in the sun - like the speckled salamanders that come to pose on the concrete patio each sun-filled morning. Wake and bake!

In June we begin to reward ourselves for all the work accomplished since spring arrived. June is play time. The lake is significantly warmer than last month. Wading in, we drag our raft down a log ramp from the shoreline and into the water.

I call it *rafting* (25), but in reality the vessel is better suited to being a dock. In fact, we ultimately tie the structure to cement-filled buckets, anchor it in a deeper part of the lake, and that is where it stays until the water temperature drops enough to discourage swimming. At that time we pole it back to shore and tow it back up onto the bank. But, for the summer, we have the perfect spot away from bloodthirsty flies for sun worshipping.

The one problem with tanning for its own sake is that it demands a complete lack of physical activity. And, being a couple who would rather march in the parade than watch from the sidelines, we don't spend a great deal of time just lying in the sun.

Ergo, on dry days my partner will encourage me to participate in a multitude of outdoor games that serve to exercise the body and bolster the ego (his ego should this statement require clarification). If it's a rainy day we *throw darts* (26) or *play cards* (27) inside the cottage where he nearly always wins. When the sun explodes on the scene, we move our butts outside. We *throw horseshoes* (28) and of course, he always wins. We *play washer toss* (29) which he wins quite a lot. We swing at the birdie, *playing badminton* (30) and . . . wait a minute. I'm really good at this. Victory is mine!

I get such a boost from my win that I don't mind getting a little dirty in the garden again. You just can't let the weeds win when you wage war against them. In fact, the earlier you start *weeding* (31), the less work it becomes. There, now my existence is justified. Jay has also found something to do, which I so appreciate that I forgive him for all the gloating he's done during game time.

That chore of which I am so appreciative is *checking the hound for fleas* (32). I am horribly allergic to these warm weather pests, much more so than black flies and mosquitoes. One bite can keep me in agony, and dusted in Gold Bond, for a solid week. Hence, my darling is diligent in keeping home and cottage flea free. I'm sure our hound dog appreciates it too.

Admiring my handiwork, I find that the garden is pretty weed free and I've also managed to *hoe* (33) out a new bed alongside the onions where I believe a row of Marigolds would look lovely. Early June, or past the risk-of-frost time period, is when the seedlings we nurtured all spring can go into outdoor beds. Inside, I take off my bug-net stockings and put myself to bed. It's been a long day – the longest day of the year in fact – and we need to *rest* (34). We've been busy as beavers, and summer has barely begun.

I love to swim in the nude and roam around the house in the nude.
You're just as free as a bird! ~ Bettie Page

July

Chapter Five

Past the longest day of the year, we're into July and the lake water is lovely and warm. The *swimming* (35) is glorious. It seems that skinny dipping is an activity which most of the planet's population has indulged in. Through research, I have discovered that among those who embrace this form of naturism there are reams of famous people. The list includes actors, artists, authors, comics, inventors, models, pinup queens, religious figures, singers (take a breath), ex-presidents et al.

How cute is this? John Quincy Adams, '*each morning got up before dawn, walked across the White House lawn to the Potomac River, took off his clothes and swam in the nude. Then he returned to the White House to have breakfast, read the Bible and run the country.*'

You see, virtually everyone has done it! So, it came as quite a shocker one day when my husband spoke up, halfway across the lake, and revealed his concern for a particularly vulnerable body part . . . one that, unclothed, tends to dangle like a worm while he's swimming (Jay thought I should change the word 'worm' to 'snake' but I convinced him that snakes don't dangle – they lay motionless in wait for prey to pass by. Besides, snakes are not known to make good bait. Worms are). Editorial rights, author's prerogative, call it what you will, the worm stays . . . the saga continues.

Hubby's unexpected anxiety over the wellbeing of his manhood stems from the sighting of one rather large female snapping turtle. He caught a glimpse of her under the dock a few months back and had forgotten about the scare she gave him. Suddenly he wonders if there's danger involved in swimming with turtles. Now really!

Still, to allay all fears of being bitten by a lurking hard-shelled reptile, I use all of my journalistic training and expertise in research tools to prove incontestably the absence of danger in swimming in turtle infested waters. Google – click . . . OMG!

Snapping Turtle Bit Boy's Penis
6/24/2005 | Staff Writers

Police divers are hunting a snapping turtle that bit a 15-year-old boy on the penis in an alpine lake. They believe the turtle had probably been dumped in the lake at Grossweil, in Bavaria, by its owner after it got too big for its tank . . . Snapping turtles can reach a weight of six stone and live for 80 years, but police believe that if they failed to catch the latest turtle escapee it will not survive through the winter when the lake freezes over.

This report is the closest I found to being an actual attack. Still, the victim wore swimming trunks . . . and lived in Europe! Apparently, Europeans are oblivious to the fact that in the snapping turtles' native homeland, North American lakes freeze over on a regular basis.

Just as I thought: there has never been a recorded incident of a snapping turtle actually biting off a worm-like appendage that dangles from a naked male body while he swims across a lake. It's perfectly safe. Hubby wants to know what I mean by 'a recorded incident.' Have there been unrecorded incidents of turtles snapping men's private parts off? I think not.

Reasonably assured, he still swims nude across the lake with me. Though I can't help but notice a rather substantial increase in the speed in which he manages to accomplish this once leisurely activity.

Note of interest: *Michael Phelps, once the fastest human swimmer on the planet, had a best speed of just under 5 MPH (during the 2008 Olympics).*

A further note of interest: *Snapping turtles can swim upwards of 15 MPH.*

Yikes! Swim faster little worm, swim faster . . .

We adore the lakes, but Nova Scotia, being Canada's ocean playground (says so right on our license plates) also has an abundance of salt water, which is perfect for *sailing* (36) in our catamaran. Jay takes care of the jib and jibing, while I keep an eye out for aquatic birds and sea creatures. Seals and seagulls are always plentiful, a joy to watch. We know they don't mind that we are naked as jaybirds. We bask and bobble in the sun on the wild Atlantic Ocean letting all our worries wash out to sea.

Only one thing can disturb this moment of serenity. It appears as a pair of 435 horse power motors attached to our ever-efficient Canadian Coast Guard, coming to check us out, to see if we are stranded . . . in need of provisions, drinking water, clothing?

'Yes sir, we do have swim suits with us and sunscreen. Yes ma'am, and drinking water . . . yes, thank-you for looking out for us. By the way, just how powerful are those Federal Government issued binoculars? Yes of course, that's a very high power indeed.'

'Have a nice day!'

The lesson here is not to keep covered, but to keep your cover close, as there will always be those among us who can see farther and move faster than we can.

Speed and nudity together do not necessarily make bad bed mates. It's just that being in the raw produces such an easy, relaxed state that I find it more conducive to slow moving activities. Still, there are a few things we do that require a certain amount of raucous speed to elicit the best outcome. To me, *water skiing* (37), performed naked at breakneck speed, is about as exhilarating as it gets.

Again, living on an ocean playground has its advantages. If you don't have access to one with lots of private coves and inlets to strip down in, you may find a large 'off-the-grid' lake that you can rip around on. You may also find that water-skis are a hard thing to master. In which case, inner tubes sweep across the water quite nicely. And, when you bounce up and down on rubber with your bare tush, it's less likely to leave a bruise.

Back on shore we slow down the pace again and engage in a little *beachcombing* (38). I'm always on the lookout for that illusive message-in-a-bottle, but thus far my creel cradles the usual assortment shore debris like seashells, pebbles and pieces of colored glass ground smooth. An intriguing shape in driftwood catches my husband's eye and though it won't fit in the creel, I just know he'll drag every inch of it home to enhance it with a little carving.

'A mermaid . . . really?'

'Well, I kind of see a womanly shape there, but I'm not sure about that third boob honey. Oh sure, I'll watch Total Recall again with you when we get home.'

Jay can catch some inspiration from tri-tit woman and I'll *get some* from Arnold Schwarzenegger.

We end this sun-drenched, water-packed month back at the cottage with an activity that makes all other aquatic sports pale in comparison. Put your snorkel and flippers on (nothing more) and dive in. Oh joy! *Snorkelling* (39), in either fresh or salt water, is always an adventure. You are guaranteed to discover something you've never seen before, each and every time you do it.

'Oooh, look at that gigantic school of minnows dashing away. And lookie there – springs from an old camp mattress! Oooh, and look! What's moving over there by those long weeds . . . is that a baby turtle? This means there must be a momma and a fertile papa turtle swimming somewhere in the lake . . . at 15 miles per hour! Oh no!'

A jittery Jay heads for shore looking for something useful to do. The camp grass has gotten longer than he normally lets it grow. We can't see the heinous thorns that inhabit the vines that snake through it on the ground.

'Are you wearing your rubber boots honey?'

With just a few more cracks at *weed whacking* (40), the grass should lay low until next spring. Revved up, the gas powered monster chews the coarse ground cover into an innocuous flat green mat.

Meanwhile, I flick off my flippers and spark up the *barbeque* (41). I believe it's been three months since the oven has been turned on, which puts me instead in front of a blazing grill to get the cooking done. My apron stays folded clean and tidy in a kitchen drawer. It's way too hot for clothing of any kind still.

I was thinking of something really cool to do in the nude for July, but that changed the day after my husband weed whacked the camp grass . . . in flip flops. Camp grass hides a vine that is particularly thorny (I may have mentioned its heinousness) to which Jay is particularly allergic.

Five years earlier he had been hospitalized and endured hours of intravenous antibiotic drip into a vein in his arm before being released. Apparently, a single thorn in a toe, picked up whilst weed whacking, can cause painful blistering of the entire foot and send a red line of blood poisoning coursing up the leg . . . every time!

Back from the hospital, round two (I'm torching his flip flops), I send hubby to *convalesce* (42) in the nude on a hammock, well above the cutting tools and the camp grass. He may yet get the meaning of self-preservation. He's a man – he can change.

Who am I kidding? I add a new first aid kit to the list of things to bring on our next outing to the cottage, with a tourniquet and an extra tube of antibiotic ointment just for good measure.

We end July at the cottage with my favorite thing to do in the nude on a clear pastoral night – *star gaze* (43). Lying on a sleeping bag on the dock, we stare up into space mesmerized by the sheer beauty and brilliance of a gazillion stars that grace the night sky.

I come from a country where you don't wear clothes most of the year. Nudity is the most natural state. I was born nude and I hope to be buried nude.
~ Elle MacPherson

August

Chapter Six

The days are becoming noticeably shorter as we move into August. By the second blue moon, feathery cool breezes have replaced the heavy hand of humidity. A slight chill pricks the night air. A bonfire right about now would be nice. The mosquitoes slink away as darkness falls making it safe to doff our duds and *dance* (44) in the firelight.

Maybe it's the native in me, but dancing naked around the bonfire is just about the most fun you can have on a star filled Saturday night . . . off a country road, on a rural lake, beside a secluded cottage.

We wake early to the sound of rustling leaves and thoughts of wind play. Jay strips down a young alder and fashions two branches into a sturdy cross. Adding a slice of thin nylon, a ball of kitchen string and a notched stick, the semblance of a quite aerially adept kite is soon apparent. *Kite flying* (45) in the raw is most comfortable mid-day when you're more likely to have the warming rays of the sun on your back.

All fun aside, it's August and the wild blueberries are ripe for the picking. We'll combine *hiking* (46) with *berry picking* (47) here as they complement each other. You have to hike into the bush to get to the berries after all. Why be hindered with clothing? All you really need is a good pair of rubber boots and a couple of clean gallon-sized ice cream buckets. Well off the beaten path, away from prying eyes, we take advantage of all the nude tanning opportunities we can find. In a few short months they'll be scarce as hen's teeth.

I am going to digress here and skip back to a hot day in southern British Colombia where I spent one summer *panning* (48) for gold on the Similkameen River. It was another brief time in my life that I had no qualms about running around naked. I had set up the perfect panning spot alongside the Platinum King, a former mine site that sees little in the way of people – clothed or otherwise.

Conveniently, the loggers and the miners had vacated making it an extremely private location. Having said that, had the King been blessed with animation, he would have chuckled one morning seeing me, bent over up to my calves in the icy, glacier-fed river, peering into the water, wearing nothing but a pair of swimming goggles . . . with four tank-sized forest rangers standing back on next to my tent. I'm not sure how long they were there, but by the time one cleared his throat to indicate their presence, the redness had set in to both sets of my cheeks.

Turns out, I needed to be warned about a gun toting male who had last been seen heading up one of the logging roads that crisscrossed the mountain on which I stood . . . naked! Just thought I should know. I assured them I had ample protection with me including two big dogs (where were those yellow bellies?) and three sound firearms. I spent the rest of the day wearing a Remington shotgun and hunting shaggy mane mushrooms. Much to my delight, along with the edible fungi, I discovered a plethora of wild huckleberries. Yummy, yummy berries . . .

Which brings us back to present day. You just know the mason jars are coming out now. *Making jam* (49) is hot and thirsty work. Boiling, stirring, ladling . . . it can't get any hotter can it? I keep a dishtowel handy and oven mitts, but forget the apron (may as well be dressed in a snowsuit). The only thing I have on is the fan. Well, that and a quart of Sangria steeping on ice in a big glass jug.

Drink up, because the thirsty work has just begun. It's late August and soon it will be time to begin the *harvest* (50). Cucumbers, tomatoes, peas, beets, carrots, onions and garlic are all dug up or picked on a warm dry day. The grapes are starting to blush and will soon be ripe for the picking as well. Keeping hydrated is important, so there's a lot of liquid consumption going on. Once the crop is in, we'll be ready to *celebrate* (51) with another bonfire. And yes, there will be dancing. Cheers!

The freest people I know are those who have the least to hide, defend or protect. Naked is powerful. ~ *Alan Cohen*

September

Chapter Seven

Sublime September – summer's end, the beginning of fall. We absolutely adore the weekends in September. Most are dry, bug free and loaded with stuff to do. A last swim in the lake – the first taste of pickles. The garden is all in and the beets and pickling cucumbers need to be bottled in brine and processed in a hot bath. No matter. It's a cool day with a stiff breeze. The kitchen is boiling, the cook is limp.

That's why it is mandatory to complete the chore without clothing of any sort. The most I concede to is a kerchief or hairnet worn on the head. Sanitation should always be kept in mind whilst handling food and especially when we *make pickles* (52). I learned in a food safety course that a single washed hair can provide the breeding grounds for 20 million pathogens in one 24 hour period. Can you say 'botulism' boys and girls?

Good, but this is supposed to be a fun read, not too didactic, and not just a load of fluff. In fact, throughout the text you'll find, I'm sure, some very interesting, if not educational, tidbits of information. And for those still counting, *reading* naked is number (53) on the list.

This is also the month that courses in schools, colleges, universities and other channels to higher education typically begin. Tying into reading, quite nicely then, is *studying* (54) . . . naked of course. Had I the time back, I would have endeavoured to do all my academic studies sans clothing. I'll even go as far as suggesting you study naked in a room that is bare of any unnecessary décor. Bare floor, bare walls, bare body – covered windows. Now what's left to distract you from that gigantic, weighs-more-than-a-microwave, sticky note plastered textbook? Not so much, thank-you.

There, you probably feel smarter already. Unless, it's your bare ass that smarts from sitting on a hard, cold floor. So bring in a pillow, but nothing fancy . . . no funky patterns, buttons, or tassels of distraction. And watch out for stuffing. Anyone who has ever had a goose quill stuck in their butt will know exactly what I'm talking about. Now the rest of you do too.

All this learning is tiring of course and you do need to get out for a well-deserved break on occasion. A *drive* (55) in the country then is one way to shake loose the many morsels of information you diligently digested. Henceforth, they will fall into a smooth, cohesive shit pile when put to paper for that nerdy professor in the Austin Powers zoot-suit. Class dismissed. There is other work to be done.

The weekends that we go to the cottage now are used to retrieve wood that is chopped and seasoned. We *pile wood* (56) into the truck each trip, return home and pile it into the garage for use in the fireplace over the winter months. There's nothing funny about this chore. It is hard work and time consuming. But, if you want a good chuckle, Google the joke about a job for a pilot and a wood cutter. Trust me, you'll laugh.

Seriously though, fall is the time of year that many of the bushes and a few of the ornamental trees can use a good *pruning* (57). Jay does all of the tall tree trimming as, for the most part, I am vertically challenged and have a terrible fear of heights.

Now, it has occurred to me that what I'm afflicted with is a fear of ladders rather than a fear of anything higher than my bellybutton. I say this as there was a time when I became stuck rooftop for a full half hour, unable to muster the courage to climb down one. I had gone up the ladder to clear a clogged rain gutter. A neighbor finally came to my rescue, holding the vile apparatus so that I could safely descend.

That being said, I have had no problem jumping from a perfectly functional aircraft flying 4,000 feet above a jump zone when learning to skydive. It's nonsensical isn't it!

With all the pruning done we head to the cottage and take to the lake for some downtime. My husband suggests taking a spin around in the rowboat. It's too cool for swimming and it's a little choppy for kayaking, so I agree. Having him *row* (58) the boat naked is a treat for me. There is a good deal of physical exertion associated with rowing a boat . . . muscles pulled taut, sweat glistening on bulging pecs, push – pull, push – pull . . . a sweaty, sultry rhythm ensues. Rowing a boat naked is hard work – I could sit and watch it for hours!

Satisfied with a long, hard workout on the water, we return to the dock and find Blue scratching at his rear end. The burrs stuck in his fur tell us he has been running through the woods, chasing bunnies most likely. This is a good time to check our canine friend for ticks.

Checking the dog for ticks (59) is actually something that we do on a regular basis in cottage country. There are lots of trees and shrubbery. We assume that there are also lots of ticks. However, as of yet, we have never found even one tick on our hound. This is a good thing, because ticks can carry potentially dangerous diseases, such as Lyme's, which can render the body useless and be quite hard to diagnose and to get rid of. Tis good to be tick-less.

Sometimes I like to run naked in the moonlight and the wind, on a little trail behind our house, when the honeysuckle blooms. It's a feeling of freedom, so close to God and nature. ~ Dolly Parton

October

Chapter Eight

October is a scary month. The sun's heat has lost most of its intensity and the hours of darkness now exceed those of daylight quite noticeably. There are not too many occasions from here to spring that we are able to engage in clothes-free activities outside. Inside, it's a different story.

Halloween will soon be here so on my agenda is the *sewing* (60) of costumes for the party that we shall no doubt attend. Sewing while naked comes with a bit of trepidation and a lot of awareness. Knowing where the scissors lay and the location of all the pins and needles is a must for safety sake. I've made many costumes over the years, but a human pincushion is one that has only been made on one occasion. It wasn't planned, it wasn't fun, and it wasn't pretty. Boo-hoo.

Seeing me wrapped up in a sewing quandary about the color of thread to choose for my project, hubby is inspired to do some dental hygiene. He likes his *floss* (61) the way he likes to be most of the time . . . naked. No stick, no wax, no minty flavor.

With his teeth clean as a whistle and me immersed in my sewing project, Jay decides to provide me with a little musical entertainment. He's *playing an instrument* (62), a trumpet that he once mastered in junior high school (says he). Apparently, unlike riding a bike, this is one activity that is not easily picked up once it's laid down. Actually it's quite scary.

Less than satisfied with his musical aptitude, he switches out the trumpet for an equally lethal instrument and challenges me to a shootout. We enjoy *target shooting* (63) immensely given that neither of us has the heart to actually kill a living animal. I am, however, able to accurately shoot a rifle, a pistol and a stream of profanities when my aim is jeopardized by a sore loser poking me in the bare bum with the butt of his 30-30.

Thankfully he has other redeeming qualities and one of these he acquaints me with regularly on Thanksgiving. In fact, I don't think he enjoys any cooking ritual as much as he does in *stuffing the turkey* (64) for our holiday meal. Interestingly, his nakedness doesn't send up any red flags as proper hygiene would normally warrant. After all, he is a smoothie, shaves everything above the thigh line and bites his nails down to the quick. There's just nowhere for those creepy little germs to hide.

'Go ahead – stuff it baby!'

Some hours later we *eat* (65) our fill, and *give thanks* (66) for the bounty and fulfillment in our lives. Life is good. Naked . . . life is great thank-you!

Party time and the tree costumes I made are looking good and leafy.

'That's a mighty fine trunk you have there sweetheart.'

I'll go out on a limb and say they're the most authentic costumes I've ever sewn. Not that they would *scare someone* (67) to pieces or anything. But, standing still in the middle of a dog park wearing one could cause an appreciable amount of anxiety.

We've had a safe and uneventful month for all the daring activities we've engaged in. We end Halloween night by running in the woods among the trees stripping off our costumes with naked abandon. Or, roughly translated, we abandon our costumes and run naked in the woods. Leaving nothing to chance, we're prompted on our return home to diligently *check partner for ticks* (68). Finding one would be really scary. Tickity-Boo!

What spirit is so empty and blind, that it cannot recognize the fact that the foot is more noble than the shoe, and skin more beautiful than the garment with which it is clothed? ~ Michelangelo

November

Chapter Nine

It's full out fall. The deciduous trees have changed their foliage to hues of red and gold. Next month, except for the modest beech tree, appearing to be clad in scraps of brown paper bag all winter long, the trees will be naked. Good for them!

But, we can't go around all fall and winter with no clothes on. Can we? Well, actually we can. We just finished stacking the last of the firewood into the garage, so we have ample heat.

You will heat your home in some fashion as well if you live in a climate where there are four distinct seasons: black fly, summer, fall and cold-as-a-witch's-tit. If you're lucky enough to live near the equator of course you'll have just two seasons: hot and wet.

By November I have a list of things I want to accomplish over the colder months. Make that two lists . . . mine and my husband's: the 'honey-do' list.

'Honey . . . do *make* me *a* new *playlist* (69) for my Nano-shuffle . . . something up-beat!'

It's cool enough to start running again and I have a hankering to take along some new tunes. Not that I couldn't do this myself. It's just that when it comes to remembering songs and the artists who sing them, I have a hard time. My memory it seems is much like my stature; it's good, but it's short. Mr. D.J. on the other hand has a memory like a bear trap: rigid, unyielding and, at times, just a little fuzzy.

So, while Jay gets down and funky recording music in the raw, I dig out my knitting needles and yarn basket. *Knitting* (70) is a great pastime that rewards your efforts in sweaters you'll never wear and dish cloths that shrink into oblivion. Thankfully, everyone likes to receive hand-knit sweaters as gifts and you can never have enough disintegrating dish cloths now can you?

Feeling a little ahead of the game in the making of presents (we also give away many jars of jam and pickles), I take some time to *surf the Web* (71) to locate a new wine recipe for our grapes. Jay says if we leave them on the vine till the first frost we can *make ice wine* (72), a delicious change of trek from our usual route.

Not that I could ever tire of my Dad's fail-free recipe. My only complaint was that some of his wine was too 'green.' Patience and proper aging are necessary for a truly good batch. There were many a year my sisters and I would stash away a bottle or two just to make sure we had some of the good stuff for a holiday meal.

While I'm busy surfing, my husband has taken it upon himself to *phone a friend* (73), Darryl, to solicit firsthand information on the art of wood carving. It had been an innocent observation that all his time spent *whittling* (74) long pieces of willow into nothing more than woodchips and kindling, could have been used to fashion us with some pretty fine hiking poles.

'Lift your phone screen a little higher sweetheart . . . you're on Skype.'

'You're welcome Darryl.'

Satisfied with my Internet quest I turn to find, to my chagrin, Blue pawing at a loose braid on his oval mat that I made a few years back. Upon further investigation I decide that the whole affair is just too ratty for a dog and quite beyond repair. If I begin to *hook a rug* (75) for him now, there will be one less present to make come the holidays. I'll *recycle* (76) the hemp fibre from the rug, along with three years' worth of saved clothes dryer lint, for a later project.

Darkness will soon appear and the day has passed with little physical exertion. A cold drizzle slips in as the sun slinks away, thwarting our plans for an evening run.

No matter. I have a backup plan. Keeping abreast of current *exercise* (77) trends, I had bought an instructional Zumba CD and am now eager to try it out.

'You can lose the jock strap sweetie . . . this won't hurt your junk - I promise.'

Salsa, samba, mambo, the merengue . . . shake it, shake it!

'*Zumba* (78) baby!'

I enjoy nakedness. I am a bit of a naturist at heart. ~ *Pope John Paul II*

December

Chapter Ten

'What time is it honey?'

'Dark.'

'Oh, 4:30. . . You sound like you have SAD already.'

SAD stands for seasonal affective disorder, a depressive state brought on by the diminishment of sunlight hours during the interminably long winter months. Or as we like to call it – 'sucks after dark'.

It's the shortest day of the year. This month has been consumed thus far with activities prompted by custom and civility. We've *signed and sent greeting cards* (79), did some *seasonal decorating* (80), and *baked* (81) dozens of shortbread cookies. Mmm . . .

Gingerbread baking in the oven emits an aroma that envelops the kitchen like a warm hug. Nothing lifts a mood quicker. And, nothing puts a damper on that mood like my husband telling me it's not to be eaten. Jay has a 'how to' book. In this case, it is 'How to' *build a gingerbread house* (82). Well, I refuse to pout. The only thing he's wearing is a smile as he turns the pages in search of the optimum design. I have a happy-pappy again!

'Yes, I can make the mortar.'

'We're out of icing sugar.'

'Really?'

Back from my excursion to the grocery store, I can't wait to shed my parka so I can curl up with Jay and Blue in front of the fireplace.

So warm, so peaceful, so sleepy, so . . .

'Who's licking me? Ears down, good boy.' Zzzz

Morning light seduces the senses, gently coaxing us from a deep slumber beneath our downy duvet. The one thing we have always done sans clothing is *sleep* (83). If, at this time, you're a beginner naturist, this is a good place to start. Take all your pyjamas, your nighties, the baby dolls you still have from the sixties, your boyfriend's triple XL T-shirts, those boxer shorts, out of your dresser drawers and give them all to charity. You can keep your eye-mask. This we allow for shift workers and for high arctic dwellers where six months of daylight at a stretch is the norm. Start now, and by spring you'll have the art of sleeping naked mastered. Truly, there's nothing to it! Pun intended.

Flushed and awake, we scamper downstairs to our little spruce tree. It's all trussed up with popped corn, homemade dingle bells, jingle balls and holly. We sit cross-legged on the floor and exchange our presents. Blue sits expectantly, tail tapping on the hardwood in triple-time rhythm. Merry, merry, merry . . . happy, happy, happy!

I love my hand-carved hiking pole, and Jay is delighted with the new pillow-embedded hammock that I secretly fashioned for him out of recycled hemp rope and clothes dryer lint. Finally, we give our pooch a new chew toy to enjoy on his freshly hooked rug. Happy, happy, happy . . .

How idiotic civilization is! Why be given a body if you have to keep it shut up in a case like a rare, rare fiddle? ~ *Katherine Mansfield*

January

Chapter Eleven

The polar bear dip is an adventure, and an event, like no other. This is where you find hundreds of people squared off, in below zero temperatures, ready to fling themselves into an icy cold ocean on New Year's Day.

Adventure defined is an encounter with the unexpected. Apparently, nobody expects to feel the blood in their veins freeze the moment one's body encounters the frigid water. The final moment, the complete disintegration of self-preservation, the sudden insanity, culminates after hours of exhilarating and tension building anticipation.

Bang! A gun shot propels the mob into a cohesive crazed entity exploding toward the shoreline. There's no way out. Death is imminent . . .

Well, I thought they were all going to die! My sense of self-preservation is well established however, and in this instance I found no compulsion to follow my husband to heaven, to hell, nor to the ambulance (which just happened to be on standby).

That said, we're at the cottage for New Year's Day and this year the temperature outside is a balmy 42 degrees Fahrenheit. There's a naked challenge, a thin layer of ice in the middle of the lake, and there's a very good chance I can win this one.

I say that because without the crowd-induced hype and hysteria, I believe that his nibs will *not* make it past his big toe! Truly, in even moderately cold water, he's a big sissy. And, it gives me the opportunity to add another thing to do naked for my list. The *polar bear dip* (84) . . . cottage style. Bang!

Now, while my husband defrosts his big toe in a bucket of hot water, I stoke the fire in the wood stove. This is done in preparation of an activity that produces many enlightened moments in our secluded, off-the-grid cottage. *Candling* (85) is not only fun to do, it serves a wonderful purpose. Candles give us light, ambiance and sobriety. A good thing, since the ice wine we made is truly delicious. Still, if we drink too much, we risk intoxication, which may lead to the loss of good judgment, balance, and our home away from home. You've heard it before. So and so got drunk, tipped over a candle and burned the house down. Enough said.

As I empty the paraffin into a large tin bucket on the stove to melt, Jay prepares the wickery along with an assortment of small, smaller, slender and tubular shaped containers on the kitchen table. The wicks are fashioned out of bits of string and laces pulled from old clothing that no one would ever want to wear. Recycled tin is used to make containers. I'll be dipping for a while, so hubby retreats to find a tow rope for the ATV. He won't tell me why. It's a surprise.

Having a good assortment of candles setting up in the back room, I glance out the window to see what my true love is up to. There he is. There's the four wheeler, the tow rope, the cross country skis . . . the skis? This is a surprise! I would never have thought to add *snow skiing* (86) naked to the list, but if he thinks we're going to flip a quarter to see who does the towing and who skis naked behind the ATV, then I'm going to get out my two-headed coin.

Back in the cottage, while hubby thaws his buns by the fire, I disrobe and prepare the chess board for a match. *Playing chess* (87) is a game of strategy involving astute planning, infinite patience and about a gallon of hot-mulled apple cider. Ergo, I'll plan to lose quickly and be severely trounced for my win in the coin toss. Really . . . who wants to be up peeing cider all night anyway?

Come morning, with my good conscience restored, it's time to pack bags and head home. *Packing* (88) at this stage is relatively easy now that we only bring travelling clothes with us.

Coveralls and snow suits hang on hooks along the back wall for use in cold and inclement weather outside.

The cottage looks so pretty draped in snow with its necklace of icicles sparkling in the sunlight. As we depart, I can't resist the urge to finish off the last bit of film in our camera and *take pictures* (89) of this wintery wonderland. Hasta la vista Bonita!

Back at home, Jay can't wait to dive into the darkroom. There he'll *develop film* (90) that we've shot intermittently throughout the last two seasons. I'm quite fine with self-development and my technology-challenged husband really enjoys the whole lengthy process of turning out superior photography, compared to that 'digital crap' as he likes to call it. Slightly concerned about chemical burns, I offer hubby an apron as he descends into darkness for the next couple of hours.

'No? Not sure? Just in case? Well, if I hear a scream I'm opening the door and coming in!'

Click . . . out go the lights.

Very well, I have my own fish to fry – or, in this case, to mount. It's my first attempt at performing *taxidermy* (91), inspired by Wally, the singing trout that hangs on the kitchen wall in our cottage. Albeit, this one won't move its lips or swing its tail to and fro, or make me smile and tap my toes to Bob Marley singing *Don't Worry, Be Happy*.

This is a trophy fish. My husband caught the 40 inch flounder in the fall and I flash froze it as soon as possible in preparation of the chance to stuff it.

As you now know, I'm given little opportunity to stuff things, having a man who holds dominion over this mostly kitchen-based activity. Why else would a perfectly sane woman save lint? So, to further quell my inner desire to stuff something – call it penis envy if you wish – I'm going to immortalize a fish.

'Hello Wanda' . . .

Clothes make the man, but nakedness makes the human being.
~ Kevin Kearney

February

Chapter Twelve

The coldest month of the year drifts in quietly, cloaking the world outside in a fresh blanket of snow. Brrrr . . . February. No matter. The fire at home is roaring and it's toasty warm inside.

I'm surrounded by stamps, ink pads, pictures, paste, ribbon and colored paper. That's right, I'm *scrapbooking* (92) . . . naked of course. The photographs hubby developed, I admit, are marvellous. I mount them in a giant album, adorning them with cute stamped catch-phrases, pretty bows and boarders.

Make memories (93) any way you like, but make them, and make them good. Then preserve them. They'll keep you smiling and in good stead well into old age. They say the memory is the first thing to go. We know better, but why take chances?

Now, the pages are full, but the larder is empty. Time to *go shopping* (94). No, not at the mall . . . that would require clothing. With today's technology and endless sources to shop on-line, you can do this in the comfort of your home in your bare buff. Just remember to wear a tad more than a smile when the UPS delivery driver pulls into your driveway at lunch time.

If the driver just happens to be your spouse, a bare smile is allowed. Why miss a golden opportunity to engage in a little *afternoon delight* (95)?

'Yes, you know I love you sweetheart. Now, please can I have the package? *Now?* Thank-you!'

The new Ellen DeGeneres Show DVDs have finally arrived and I can't wait to live, love, laugh with my favorite comedian. Not committing to the trappings of television, most of our entertainment viewing comes in the form of these magical plastic discs that come alive with a click of a mouse.

I highly recommend *watching comedy shows* (96) in the raw, coupled with unbridled laughter and a box of Kleenex. At my age, unbridled laugher sometimes results in tears of joy and on occasion, accidental squirts of pee (the bladder is actually the first thing to go). Hence, the Kleenex. As such, I have to agree with Loretta LaRoche's statement from her book, *Life is Short – Wear Your Party Pants*: " . . . there's a very short distance between tears and laughter – they both offer relief."

I also agree with her metaphoric title which incidentally has nothing to do with wearing clothing. Its intention is to help people "find ways to become more relaxed, and embrace joy instead of anxiety and pain."

Just remember that laughter truly is the very best medicine for whatever ails you. You can lose the pants anytime!

As evening wanes, the moon and stars begin to dance across the thick bed of snow that lingers on our back lawn. Come spring, come warmth, come birds and bugs, come longer days and shorter periods of darkness, the snow will melt into oblivion.

This may be the last chance of the year to *make snow angels* (97). By moonlight, falling backwards naked into a patch of freshly fallen snow is a beautiful thing. Jay and I lay back staring into each other's smiling eyes, swishing our arms up and down to form our angel wings. Watching . . . waiting, to see who will be the first to bolt for the patio door. All it takes is one nanosecond of lost eye contact and . . . zoom, zoom. Can that man run!

'Okay, it's still cold out! Open the door – honey!! . . . please!!!'

Promising jam and honey on it, I plead my way back inside. Warm and cozy again by the fireplace, I spread a large foam mat out on the floor and we proceed to fill in the pieces. Puzzle pieces that is.

Puzzling (98) naked is another one of those great pastimes that rewards your efforts with something fairly useless, yet allows one to forget all the stresses of life in general. On this occasion the puzzle we're working on depicts the giant face of a polar bear. That's a lot of white. Who da thunk there were that many shades of white?

'Here's the last corner piece sweetheart. I'll work on the tongue.'

But first, I'll get my husband an icepack for his arm. I swear that bruise is getting bigger by the minute. All kidding aside, there are so many cool things to do without the encumbrances of clothing, that I'm having a hard time deciding what to include in the completion of my list.

Writing (99) naked is a given. I do that all the time. Seeing me in this quandary, Jay comes to sit beside me and softly strokes my hair. *Sharing moments of intimacy* (100) suddenly comes to mind. These moments needn't include talk, sex or fondling of any sort. They're just special times when without a word, a touch, or a stitch of clothing, you feel as one, you are complete, you're where you belong . . . at just that moment.

But don't *wait* for special moments. Go out and get them. Seize the day, take that mountain, do it all. Just remember to do it all – or as much as common sense and decency allows – naked! As for myself, hubby and our hound, we're off to a secluded island, on a Greek *retreat* (101), far away from work and worries, from hearth and home, from fur-clad barbarians . . .

~ The End ~

About the author

Catherine Roberts is a freelance journalist now living, loving and laughing near her sons and grandson in beautiful British Columbia, Canada. *101 Things to do Naked! A Guide to 'Dress-Free' Living* is her first published book of humour. It won't, however, be her last! ☺

About the illustrator

Mike Dominic is a freelance artist living in Halifax, Nova Scotia. His past illustration work has been published by Apex Books, Sketch Magazine and Penguin Books. He is a regular contributor to the Lovecraft Ezine.

In addition, he runs a small comics imprint, AIM Comics www.aimcomics.com, where he publishes print and digital editions of comics work by himself and his friends. He occasionally blogs about his art and other things at www.paladinfreelance.com.

Made in the USA
San Bernardino, CA
01 December 2019